IMMORTAL HOUNDS

2

Ryo Yasohachi

Table of Contents

Characters

Escape Artists

A dark organization that hides Vectors from the police.

Rin Kazama
A girl who has infiltrated the MPD. Called "Fuurin" by the organization. Fights in a sailor outfit.

Kiriko
Rin's "sister." Fights in a cheerleader outfit.

Mama
A mysterious woman who manages the Escape Artists' girl soldiers.

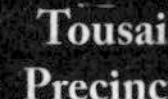

Tousai Precinct

A group of three led by Kenzaki comprises the Anti-Vector Unit.

Shin'ichi Kenzaki
Chief. His sister, Ikumi, was killed by a Vector.

Wakabayashi
Kenzaki's subordinate. Largely in charge of gathering intel.

Shigematsu
Kenzaki's subordinate despite being his elder. A great marksman. Nicknamed "Shige."

Rescue

UNDO

Short for the United Nations Disease-control Office

Kanai
Executes Vectors arrested by the police.

Remove

Vectors

A group of murderers who spread Resurrection Deficiency Syndrome (RDS). Those who love them become incapable of revival.

Teruyoshi Kouda
The Vector who killed Ikumi, Kenzaki's sister. Currently active as an Escape Artist.

Kashiwagi
A Vector debuting in this volume.

Tsutomu Takamiya
A Vector who has killed three women working night jobs. Called "Fatass" by Kenzaki.

"Snow White"
A Vector debuting in this volume. Her real name is unknown.

Previous Volume Summary

In a world in which "death" does not exist, Lieutenant Shin'ichi Kenzaki of the Tousai Precinct investigates the mystery of murders, which were previously presumed impossible. In the shadow of the crimes lurk the enigmatic organization "Escape Artists" who assist the culprits (Vectors) in eluding the law. Can Kenzaki hunt down the truth of this situation? What is the "secret of this world" which is gradually revealed?

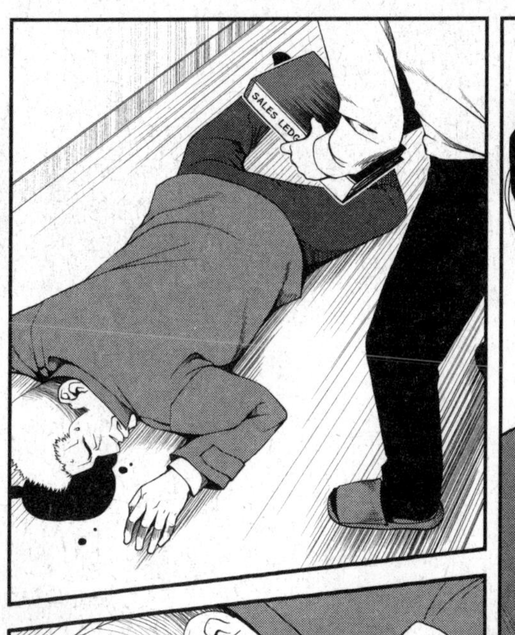
SALES LEDG

Haa
Haa
Haa
SALES LEDGER

D...
Damn you...

Haa
Haa
Haa

Run...
Kashi-
wagi.

Run,
now!
FLINCH
Ngk
...
THUP
THUP
Shit...

8

I Can't Afford to Give Up

Are you free this evening?

GLANCE
ちろっ
Uh...
キラ～ン
SPARKLE
for a get together like last time?

Uhm... I'm free, do you know whether Shige will be?
I assigned him to that case.
He should be back before long.

If the Chief doesn't have any plans, then...
NOD
コクッ
Oh, I know!

While we're at it, let's have some fun together!
HAHAHAHAHAHA
Hold on.
Huh? Do you wanna go?

Why exactly is everybody invited?

Uhm...
Why, you ask...

きら――ん
SPARKLE
Ah haaa ...
ぴきーん
TWINKLE
Oh, so that's it.

Hey, Waka-bayashi,
seems we would get in the way.
Wha ?

Just the two of us?

That's what I meant.

Whoaa !
No waay !
Fine.
I'll be done by 8.
Where should we go?
Up to you.

I'll make a reservation somewhere nice.
Dining Tour Guide
Restaurant Guide Edition
Girl's Weekly
Special Issue!
Restaurants for Dates
NOWAAAAAY!!!

DOOOM
Wait a sec!
Why the Chief?

SSFF
He doesn't talk much, his brow is always furrowed,
and is the type who shoots first and asks questions later.
For real!
Isn't he a poor match for Rin the cutie?
Can't you keep that to yourself in front of the man himself?

SPARKLE
Then
why don't we go out to eat tomorrow?
I know a great place.
SPIN
Dining Tour Guide
Restaurant Guide Editio

I decline, Sergeant Wakabayashi.
You are not my target.

But I will take the details of that place you mentioned.
... Sure.
Hee Hee Hee Hee
So lame!
Bwa ah ha ha ha ha ha ha ha!!

HOO
ふー
So that's it.
You should give it up.
I'm a boring man.

I know that.
But I can't afford to give up.

Heh.
You're a curious woman.
Vector Unit!

Oh, Kenzaki!
It seems that the Vector got away.
Shige contacted us.
Dining Tour Guide

The culprit is a lone female.
Local units are in pursuit!
Brief me in the car.
Let's go, Waka-bayashi!
Sir!

There they go.
Well, today's a bust.
Sorry. But there's always next time, Rin.
Yes.
There will be other chances.
Compose
To. Kiriko
Subject: Emergency (Protection)

Hoo
Hoo
Hoo
Where did she go?
She's gotta be close.
Search all over!
haa
haa
haa
NO PARKIN
haa
haa
haa
haa
koff
koff
BAMM

Gave us a lotta trouble.
KLAK
WHUD
Uh...
Vector apprehended.
Urgent.
ZLASH
Uh...
guah?

JAKK
KA
BLAM
BLAM
BLAM
BLAM
BLAM
ZWSH
ZWSH
KA
BLAM
BLAM
BLAM
BLAM
ZWSH
ZWSH

BAM
BAM
BAM
BAM
What ?!
BAM
BAM
An Escape Artist!
BAM
BAM
ZAASSH

Sorry!
Take care of the rest!
BANG
Shit!
WHUMP
POWW

ふー っ
SIGH
Geez.
Why did you have to go and do that?
WHIP
Oopsie.
VWUM
BAMM

You should've stayed down.
VWOOOOO
Persistent types aren't popular.
Shut yer mouth!
OO
BLAM
BLAM
!!
KA
BLAM
BLAM
SLUMP
See?
Wouldn't it have been better to just die?

ZWAPP
ZWIP
Nighty night! ★
ZWIP
TREMBLE
ガク
ガク
TREMBLE
Glad I made it in time.
Are you hurt?
SPLAT
Sorry I'm late!
Escape Artist, at your service! ♡
WINK
きゅぴん!

BLAAARGH
オロロロロロロロロロ…
DRIP
ボタ
DRIP
ボタッ

Um...? What's with that reaction?
That's pretty hurtful.
I saw something gross, can't help it. Sorry! Sorry!

Are you saying that my wink is gross?
No, no, that's not what I meant!

I mean, I can't see your face, let alone a wink.
UPF
うぷっ
Oh, that's right.

The shock might have been too much for you.
Let's get out of here.
The ruckus will make the cops come swarming.

What are you doing, Kiriko?!
Tsk.

Shut it, newbie.
What's wrong with an Escape Artist doing her job?

This wasn't what Fuurin ordered.
She told us to wait for another team's support.
I haven't called any other team.
VROOOOOOM
What?!

I'm saying that Super Kiriko can handle this alone.
All that's left of this mission is for you to pick us up.
Gun-shots!
This way?
POLICE
POLICE

Agnk!
DUCK
ひょこっ
Gaah!
BLAM
BLAM
BLAM
BLAM
BLAM

Do you really think Fuurin could make it at this point?
If she were to vanish during every case,
she would seem way more suspicious!
WHUD

Enough already.
Uhm ...
Hurry up and find a rendezvous point, Kouda.
...Roger.

I heard that somebody in a sailor uniform would...
Huh ?
Oh, so you're a fan of Fuurin, too?
YANK

BAM
Well, sure,
she's a teeensy bit better at using guns than I am.
What ?

But just a teensy bit.
Aaack!
There she is!
The female Vector!
MPD POLICE

BLAM
BLAM
BLAM
BLAM
KA
MPD POLICE
MPD POLICE

URP
But in terms of total power, Hyper Kiriko is definitely stronger!
And don't forget it.

But I'm glad.
Hmm ?
Glad that such a skilled Escape Artist came to my rescue.
Heh heh. Now you get it!
If Kiriko can pull off this debut mission with style,
I'm sure Mama will acknowledge me as a full-fledged Escape Artist.

Is there any way Ms. Sailor Uniform could come?
You just said you were glad that I was here!

Shige!

WOOO
WOOO
WOOO
P D

So you came.
Sorry, Kenzaki.
I screwed up.

I got the client list
from a veterinary medicine wholesaler.

I suspected he was a Vector, but when I checked him nothing was amiss,
but the woman who fled turned out to have a totally falsified ID and records.

There was a shady female worker there, and when I called out to her,
this man suddenly struck me from behind.

Test the man for RDS first.

I'll take care of it.

Urgent message!

It's from the crime scene.

The Escape Artists have appeared!

What?!

The shitbugs have arrived.

Relay this to all forces.

TAP

I will take command from here.

Do not allow the Vector to escape alive.

End of Chapter 8

9

My Prey

GASHAK
WHAP
BLAM
BLAM
BLAM
BLAM
Don't return fire!
It's that corner! Go around!
KRAK
ZWIP
Gah
ZZIP

BLAM
BLAM
We gotta move!
At this rate, they'll surround us!

P- Please... wait a second ...
HAA
は.
HAA
はーっ
I...I'm catching my breath...
はぁ
HAA
はぁ
HAA

Tsk.
Fine. 20 seconds.

Only ...
that long?
HAA
HAA
はっ
はっ
HAA
HAA
BLAM
BLAM
BLAM
Shit, it was a bunch of cops stupidly charging straight ahead.
Why did they suddenly switch to encirclement ?

HONK
HONK
BEEP
Even for the evening rush hour,
it usually isn't this jammed.

What are you doing, Kouda ?!
Still no pick up?
KLATCH

BIP
KLAK
KLAK
KLIK
KLIK
Uhm... Away from the traffic jam...

This girl can't hold up for much longer.
The traffic is awful ...
Maybe there's been an accident.
Don't give me that "maybe" crap!
Pick another rendezvous point!
Sorry.

AAAARGH!!

KABAMM

Why is everyone so damn useless?!

GRRRRRR
ゴゴゴゴ
Today is meant to be Kiriko's grand debut as an Escape Artist!
Why is every last bastard getting in my way?!

If I fail during a mission I chose on my own,
Mama will scold me!
ガ
ガ
ガ
KLANG
KLANG
KLANG

Then let's call for backup, Miss Kiriko.
Shut up!
Just hurry up and find a better spot!
Uhm ...

くるっ
SPIN
A coworker told me this, but ...

during the evening rush, it's quicker to take a detour over the river,
even if it's a more roundabout way.

Over the river?
You mean, cross the bridge?
Yes.

Well, Kouda?
Ah... Well, the traffic is moving faster that way.

We'd be able to rendezvous faster.
But...

The bridge is risky.
If we're attacked, there's no escape route.
I-Is that so...

Hmm...

If they're getting picked up by a car,
lure them to the other side of the river.

I've asked a colleague in the traffic division to help out,
told him not to put up a checkpoint on the far bank.
I hope they fall for it!

If they try to break away they'll choose an area without traffic.
And if that's a place close by, then...

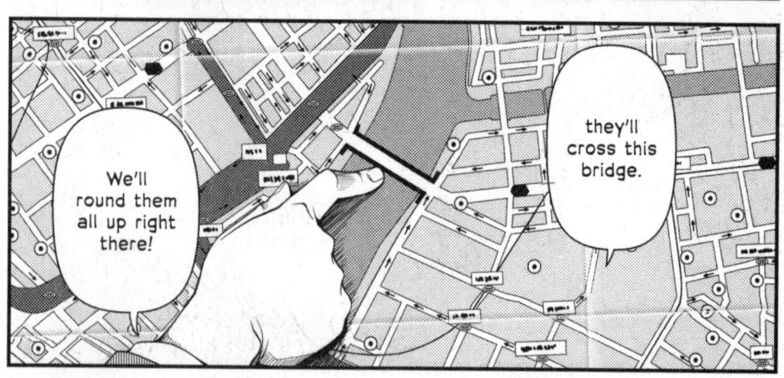
they'll cross this bridge.
We'll round them all up right there!

But, well...
we got lucky this time.

They might just hole up until the traffic settles down...
That's why the cops on the scene have them surrounded.
Roger!
Remind the team at the scene to keep the pressure on them.

They're usually just trouble-makers who cause traffic jams,

THE GOVERNMENT MUST FREE
THE DAM'S CONSTRUCTION!
DON'T DESTRO
NATURE!
he animals are crying!
Stop!
Save us!
ssociation for Citizen

POLICE
but thanks to them, the Escape Artists have nowhere to run.
How very gracious of them.
Lieutenant Kenzaki! The Escape Artists have made a move!

They have stormed the perimeter!

They seem to be heading away from the bridge!

That was almost too easy.

Huh?

A feint.

Yup.

They'll turn back to the bridge.

Wakabayashi! Head to the bridge with the reinforcements.

You can call for surrender just once.

Shoot no matter how they respond.

コクッ

NOD

What is it, Shige?
Ah, well...
LICE

...

Considering how well this plan is going,
you don't seem very happy.
Ha ha ha
HOO
ふー…っ

Can it really be this easy
to catch Escape Artists?

If it were that simple,
then we should've had no issues nabbing them before.
Hmm...
Haah,
I see.

It seems the Escape Artist you met

is a rather fascinating woman.

You've quarreled a bunch of times,

even made a deal in the Takamiya case.

If such an enemy were brought down too easily,

it'd be boring.

That's absurd.

Ah...

SFF
So that's what it is.

SKRIT
カリ
カリ
SKRIT

Contact the station!
Sir!
VWIP

Tell them to send this over ASAP.
And Shige!
Y– Yeah ...?

I have a favor to ask.
What is it this time?

HAA はぁ

HAA はぁ

はぁ HAA

はぁ HAA

Kouda! Where are you?

I'm almost at the meet-up point.

C'mon, it's only a little further. Hang in there.

HAA ゼーはーっ HAA

GASP ゼーはーっ HAA

O... Okay...

We'll be safe once we cross that bridge.

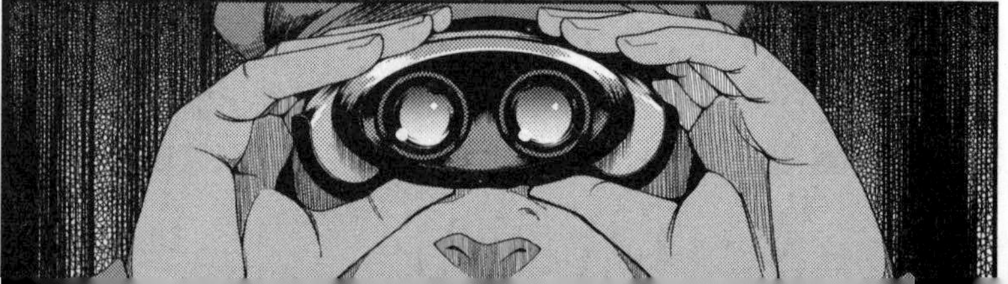

Who just fired?!
The unit on the far bank?!
N- No, it wasn't us!
Then who was it?!
BAM
BAM
BAM
BAM
BAM
GA

You came,
Fuurin ...?
Y...

I told you to call for backup.

グイッ
YANK

Are you some dumb mongrel that can't follow orders,
Kiriko ?!

Well, I can't help it!
If I don't do this,
Mama will never make me an Escape Artist.

If you're here just to play around, then go home.
Shut the hell up!
And isn't your new mission to seduce that detective ?!
あわ
あわ
FLUSTER
FLUSTER

Leave the Escape Artist job to me.
All you gotta do is act cute and flirt with that sad, slick cop!
...
My order to call for backup was an error on my part.
Lieutenant Kenzaki is my prey.
And therefore I myself should take care
of all matters he's involved with.

Something is off.

Seems our ambush has been discovered.
Let's launch an attack, Mr. Wakabayashi!
No, no. We're going to stay on stand-by.

Kenzaki's orders were to absolutely wait until they're on the bridge.
Besides, see how their faces are obscured?
MPD POLICE

The new arrival is probably another Escape Artist.
The chance of anything other than an ambush working is close to zero.

The Escape Artists are turning back!
They won't approach the bridge!
It failed.
Let Kenzaki know. We'll wait for his orders.

The bridge was a trap?
They were gonna ambush us?

In this case, I would set a trap on the bridge.
Which means Lieutenant Kenzaki set a trap.

Wait a sec.
That's your only reason?
A hound would get it.
You don't yet under-stand, Kiriko.

Stop treating me like I'm a kid!
Uh... Uhm...!
How are we going to escape without crossing the bridge?

Oops.
HALT
ピタッ
GRIK
ギッ

We'll cross a bridge.

Wait, wait.
You're the one who told us not to cross!

There's a bridge where the police can't set a trap, and past which there's no traffic.
Where the hell is that ?!
ギャース
RAAAWR

A bridge of people.

ENTERPRISES
THE RIVER IS CRYING
RETURN THE MOUNTAINS, RETURN THE RIVER!
Hear our voices!
DON'T ALLOW THE DESTRUCTION OF NATURAL RESOURCES!

If we charge through the crowd,
the police can't touch us.

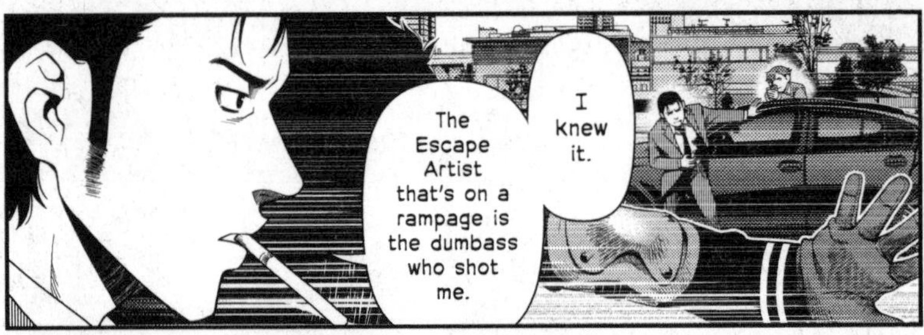

End of Chapter 9

10
Regret and Suffering

HUB
BUB
BUB
HUB
HUB
BIND VOICE

BUB
HUB
HUB
Is that cosplay?
The hell are they thinking?
BUB
HUB
BUB
This isn't that sort of event.
Huh? Isn't it hard to see their faces?

Hey, Fuurin,
I think we've overstayed our welcome in this protest.
I'm aware.
We've covered enough distance.

GACHAK
It's about time to start.
Ain't you a pair of cuties?
What anime are you from? Or is it a game?

But if you're playing around, could you do it elsewhere?

I'm getting embarrassed just looking at you.

Oh, knock it off.

くすくす GIGGLE

ガガガガガガガガガ BLAM BLAM BLAM BLAM BLAM BLAM

WAAAAAAH

BANG
BANG
BANG
Go, Kiriko!
Stop ordering me around!

Y-You don't need to go so far just to save me.
Whew...
Don't say such dull crap!

"A phan-tom killer!"
BLAM
BLAM
"He's shooting at us, run!"
BLAM
BLAM
BLAM
BLAM

"There's a random shooter on the loose" ...
Huh?
There's a gun!
Run!
TROMP
TROMP
TROMP
You'll be shot!

TROMP
TROMP
What's going on?
Hey —
TROMP
TROMP

What's going on?
You're running the wrong way!

Uhm...
For real?

If the Escape Artist is a hound like me,
then she'll conceal herself among the panicked herd of sheep.
That was my theory, but...
BANG
POLICE

Finding her this easily
seems like a love story. Makes me wanna puke.

Love stories don't suit hounds.
Let's put an end to it here.
GASHAK

ZISSH
Don't mind the civilians!
Fire every bullet you've got!
CURRY

Shit!

THUD
THUD
THUD
THUD

That bitch.
As over-the-top as always.

BLAM
BLAM
BLAM
BLAM
ガガガガ

GA
BLAM
BLAM

BLAM
BLAM
BLAM
BLAM
BLAM
GA
BANG
BANG
BLAM
BLAM
BLAM
BLAM
GA
BLAM
BLAM
BLAM

ZAA
SSH

So strong ...
Retreat! Let's regroup!
Idiots, don't pull back now!
BLAM
BLAM
BLAM
Go, Kiriko!
On it!
GA
BANG
BANG
BANG
BANG
BANG
BANG
BANG
BANG
Tch!

Drop the woman you're carrying !!
JA-AKK
POWW
BANG
BANG
BANG
BANG
BANG
BANG
RRY HOUSE
oCo ICHIBANYA

SLUMP
ガクッ
Kiriko, don't wait for me!
Once you've met up with the car, escape with the Vector!
Got it!

BAASH

HFF

Tch
A sniper?

GABLAM
BLAM
BLAM
BL

Shige, can't you shoot the escaped Vector?
Sorry! Can't do it now!
KLANG
KLANG
KLANG
KLANG

And I've never shot a moving target!
After them!
Yes sir!
BAANG
Gah

Kouda, can we rendezvous yet?
Almost there. Keep going!

Uhm... Miss Kiriko...? Can I ask you a question?
What?!

Do you know what happened to the manager
who helped me escape?
Oh, that's right.
The organiza-tion had a message for you.

Congrats on earning a point.
You now have 2 points in total.

Oh, no...
I guess he was taken to the protection facility.
Seems he was arrested for aiding your escape.

S- So...
you mentioned this earlier, but...

that person in the sailor outfit,
is she trying to give somebody RDS, like I was?
Not only that, she's been told to kill the man once she infects him.
What a nasty mission, right?

どんっ
SHOVE
But this isn't the time to talk abou—
Oof!

WHUMP
ドサッ

VROOM
ブォーン
SKREE
キュ
キュ
キュ
SKREE
SKREE
タ
タ
タ
THUP
THUP
THUP

Sorry for the wait, Kiriko!
SKREEE
キキッ

Kiriko ...?
What are you doing?
That's what I'd like to know.
UURRGH...
ぐぬぬ…

BANG
BANG
BANG
HIBIYA LINE
Ken-zaki,
we're out of bullets ...
ZWIP
Shit.
GASHAK
BANG
BANG
BANG
BANG
To think, after all of this, they're gonna get away...
Hmm?
BANG
BANG
You can't do this!!

To make him love you, only to kill him?!
You can't do something so sad!
Using love as a tool for murder is wrong!
Kenzaki, isn't that the Vector?
Hold on.
I felt nothing but regret and suffering afterwards!
What are you doing?
Let's stop doing such foolish things!

BANG

BANG

BANG

BANG

WHUMP

GRIK
Hey, Escape Artist,
what was that little speech about?

Abso-
lutely no
idea.
Failing to
complete
a mission
like this
is
unpleas-
ant.
PLINK

VWAASH

Regret
and
suffering...
huh?

Your RDS test results have come back.
Positive.

I see.

You don't seem shocked.
Did you know that she was a Vector?
Yes. She told me herself.

When I told her my feelings for her,
she said, "If you love me, you will die,"
and, "I've already killed one person,"
and so she turned me down.

She turned you down?
Which means that you two...
Right. We hadn't so much as held hands.

And yet you still contracted RDS...
Well, I'm very sorry to hear that.

Don't pity me.
In fact, I'm happy.
Now that she's gone,
this disease is the only proof of my love for her.

BEEP
BEEP
BEEP

INTERROGATION ROOM 3
KACHAK
カチャッ
Hello?
ピッ
PIP

Oh, it's you.
What is it?

What's with that tone, Detective?
You're the one who made me memorize your number, right?

I'm finally outta the clink and thought that I'd give you a call.
How's it going?

Good timing, ya fat bastard.
I've got something to ask you, too.

End of Chapter 10

11
Are You the Spy?

モグ
MUNCH
モグ
MUNCH

GLUG
ゴッ
GLUG
ゴッ
GLUG
ゴッ

モグ
KLAK
モグ
KLAK
カチャ
MUNCH
カチャ
MUNCH

It's been nearly 30 minutes.
I didn't think they'd eat in total silence...

Rin being quiet is one thing,
but c'mon, Kenzaki, it's a first date.
haaah
You shouldn't expect that from the Chief...
And so...

why don't we consider this a date of our own?
Sorry,
you're not my type at all, Waka-bayashi!
wah ha ha ha

Humph.

They aren't obeying the very basics of a stakeout.
It seems Wakabayashi needs to be retrained.

Now then,
let's get to it.

How did you know?

About what?
Don't play dumb.
About Vectors.
CHOMP

That their aim is to spread RDS,
and that RDS spreads when a Vector loves.

Escape Artists.
HALT

We've been able to confirm both.
There's no error there.
The question is
how you came to learn that information.

This has bothered me for a while.
Why do they show up
almost every time we go to arrest a Vector?

So naturally, I suspect there is a spy lurking in the force
that's tipping off the Escape Artists.
WHAM

Are you the spy?

KLINK

RUSTLE

According to this book,
it's taboo to talk about work on a date.
ions You Can't Ask, Answered!
dult Dating
Manners and Techniques

ふーっ
SIIGH

Oh?

Look, Waka-bayashi!
Seems like they're making progress!
Oh, yeah?

Let me be clear.
I'm not interested in any of that.
I'm here today to talk to you about the Vector issue.
If you're looking for romance, try someone else.

Someone else won't do, Lieutenant Kenzaki.
There is no point if it isn't you.

That's enough.
Tell me your source for intel on Vectors.
Then let's try this:

Date me.
カチン
CLENCH

Like I just said...
In exchange, I will tell you everything.
KLATTER

Every-thing...?

Yes.
If you teach me love, I will tell you.

Fine.

All right.
Do as you please.

Please keep me in your favor.
Wait just a damn minute!!
ZHFF

Give it some thought, Rin!
What's there to like about a frowny machine like him?!
NOOOO

I'm not telling you to date me,
but surely there are better options!
Stop, Waka-bayashi.
Let's go.
Okay.

You aren't asking any questions.
Hmph.
I'm sure you don't plan to tell me anything until I teach you love.
That being said,
I don't really get it either.
At my age,
it's not as though I don't have experience.
But my only memories are of it being a major bother.
To be honest, I feel like love is useless.

Didn't you say before that you felt the same?

Lately,
I've had experiences that only served to confirm that stance.

Yes.

But it was for love that my sister
risked her life, and died.

Don't worry.

I'll make time for a date or whatever.

But you'll have to spill everything in return.

No.
We will not date.
I do not think it's efficient
for two people to date
when they can't grasp the concept of love.
So...
starting with actual practice would be a better idea.

Well ...?
Think you can grasp it?

No,
that didn't really stir up any deep emotions.

And I should say
the stench of cigarettes is unpleasant.

UPFFF

ゴッホン
KOFF
ゴホゴホ
KOFF
What's the matter, Lieutenant Kenzaki?
Nothing.

Perhaps it's simply that once isn't enough.
From here out, please repeat practical acts of intimacy on a regular basis.
Adult Dating
Manners and Techniques

What is it?
Did I say something strange?

Please respond, Lieutenant Kenzaki.
Was it strange?
SHAKE
ぶる
SHAKE
ぶる
Lieu-tenant Kenzaki.

12
The Start of a Serious Battle

Hold on a minute,
Kenzaki.

Is that story true?
Don't make me repeat myself.

"If you teach me love, I will tell you."
I've agreed to date Rin Kazama on that condition.

SKATEBOARDING FORBIDDEN
Highway Patrol Di
That bitch. I called with, "Are you the spy?"
And instead of folding, she raised me.
Wait, wait, wait!

That girl knew the mechanism of how RDS is transmitted.
And then for her to say, "I will tell you..."

Yes. It seems to be the case that
the spy in the force,
Rin Kazama, is a Vector.

If you screw up, you'll die of RDS!

GRAB

This is our chance, Shige.

If we're going to defeat
the Vectors and Escape Artists,
we desperately need more information.

And I can gain that from Rin Kazama through this game of love.
It's easy, right?
What's easy about risking your life ?!

Besides, it's not as innocent as a game.
Rin's the one who made the first move, right?
Which would mean...

It's proof that our investigation has hit on something vital.
GRITT

I'm well aware.
She fully intends to kill me.

Enough!
WHUD

I'm gonna slap cuffs on that girl!
C– Come on, Shige...

The theory is to allow spies to swim free.
There are three reasons not to arrest Rin Kazama.
Like I care!
If we arrest her, this nonsense will be over with.

First,
she herself told us how the RDS infection spreads.
No suspected spy would ever reveal themselves to be a spy,
and yet she purposely told us that love is the method of infection.

There was some purpose to that.
She had her own intentions.
Rin Kazama is not a hound that's simply loyal to her owners.

What intentions could she possibly have?
I don't know.
But it's very possible that I can extract more intel from her.

We should just arrest her and make her spill!
That won't work, Shige.

Arrested Vectors
are executed by UNDO within 24 hours,
and within that time frame we'd get just a few hours to rein them in.
There just isn't enough time to extract information.

That's the second reason.
Urgh ...
So it's best to let her swim.

No, no, I still can't agree.

Risking your life for a case is out of the question.
I won't allow it.

Thirdly,
because of what happened to Ikumi,
there is no way I'd ever love a Vector.

This means that I won't die.
It's a gamble with zero risk.
It's because of Ikumi that I'm refusing!

You'd better not forget,
SLAM
I was at the scene, too.

My limbs had been shot by the Escape Artists,
and, writhing around like a worm,

like you, I had no choice but to watch that girl die.

Please, no more.

Letting her swim is one thing,
but I can't condone you dating her, either.

Her promises are just lip service.
If she breaks her word and flees, then it's all over.

Spare me
from going through that again.

Teaching her "love" is a vague condition,
and to risk your life
on such an unreliable promise is totally—
She will talk.

As long as I keep my promise,
she absolutely will.
So says my intuition.

That's not exactly scientific.
If Kenzaki says so, then she'll talk.

What? Not you, too, Shige.
He's got a bloodhound's nose.
tsk

Is that how it works ...?
Hey, Waka-bayashi,
there's no need to think about it that hard.
After all, this game...

will end when I fall in love and die,
or she falls in love and talks.

That's all there is to it.
Chief ...

BEEP
GA
WHIP
SPIN
SHAK

BANG
BANG
BANG
BANG
BANG
BANG
BANG
CHAKK

GA
GRIK

Uh... Huh?
Uhm... uhm...

ゴン
WHAM
Pull the slide!
Ow!

Don't panic if it jams.
How many times do I have to tell you?

You aren't hitting the targets at all.
Are you even trying?
GASHAK
I'm sorry,
but I'm not a lefty.

JAKK
The stance that you taught me is so awkward.
Can't I shoot normally until I get the hang of it?

You're a driver, remember?
That stance is perfect for cramped car interiors.

Visualize the situation.
The police come to question you while you're standing by in the car.
M P D POLICE
M P D POLICE

One asks for your license from the driver's side
while the other hangs back about 4 or 5 yards away.

In that case, you begin the getaway.
Take out the closest cop first.

Then quickly fire at the second cop.
Then speed off to make your escape.
All in about five seconds.

Was there a scenario where you could've used the Weaver or Isosceles stances?
No...
If you get it, then get back to practice.
TRILLL
TRILLL

Some of that can't be helped.

They've lived their whole lives without touching a gun.

MPD TOUSAI PRECINCT

It was expected that training would take some time.

Well, sure, I guess.

Anyways, was that OK?

Was what OK?

The surveillance on Kenzaki's team.

All three went out, right? Maybe we should've kept a closer eye on them.

We've finished the pullout of the antibiotic route in Tokyo.
They should have no way of catching us for a while.
Bento
Special Unagi BENTO
BENTO

Right now, increasing Kouda's fighting power takes higher priority than surveillance.
I wonder ...
Hamburger Bento ¥570
¥550
¥520
Cutlet Rice ¥520
Weekly Menu

If his training goes well, I'll put in a good word for you with Mama.
Really?! I'll work super hard!

Be thorough, please.
Leave it to me!
Here you are.

If Mama catches wind that Lieutenant Kenzaki has blown my cover as a spy,
I'll be taken off of this undercover mission.

I'll keep Kiriko busy with Kouda for a while longer.
Oh, Rin!

PokaPoka Bento
Sorry for letting
Waka-bayashi butt into your date.

Max Total Cost 24-hour Parking ¥2,000
25 Min/¥200
How did it go afterwards?
Did Kenzaki agree to date you?
We are now officially dating.

I'm so happy for you!
But I'm surprised that Kenzaki agreed.
Good luck!

Right...
This is the start of a serious battle
between Lieutenant Kenzaki and me.

Here ya go!

He steam-rolled us in the end,
but will Chief be okay?
Hmph!
SNAP
PLUFF
PLUFF

Five Rules for Happiness

As if I give a damn!

That bastard won't listen no matter what we say.

① House Ramen
② Extra Large Ramen
③ Special Roast Pork Ra
④ Extra Large Roast Pork
Hours: 11:00 a.m. to 12 a.m.
Noriyan Ramen Restaurant

Our ramen's flavor is enhanced by pepper, special-grade

Well, he was never the type
to listen to our opinions.
I'm pissed off at you, too, Wakabayashi.
SLURP

Huh? What did I do?
MNCH
MNCH
I bet you think Kenzaki is cool or something, right?

Gave myself away, eh?
He's kinda mesmerizing.
Geez. That's what I mean.
SLURP

He's risking his life on an investiga-tion.
MNCH
MNCH
I've never even seen that on crime TV shows.

And if he's able to extract info from Rin,
then that'll be a huge leap forward.
You think it'll work out?
ZLURP

Won't it?
It might be a leap forward for Kenzaki,
but not necessarily for the investiga-tion.

The woman plans to straight-up kill Kenzaki.
She isn't just any Vector.

Any intel we'll be able to extract from Rin Kazama
will be something that no mere cop could handle.

In any era and place, it can be speculated that
a man who knows too much will meet an unhappy end.
CHOMP

Kenzaki is most likely prepared for whatever awaits him.
I'm nearing retirement, so I have no regrets.

But you're still young.
If this goes south, leave the team.

Don't become collateral damage.
Don't let Kenzaki influence you, no matter what.

Shige,
you're like my grandpa.
Wha ?!

Listen, you! Here I am trying to—
Being the heir and the eldest grandkid, I was spoiled.
No matter what I did, he'd always fuss over me, ask if I was OK.

You don't need to worry.
Going down with the ship isn't trendy these days.
You're being honest?
GRRR

If the going gets tough,
I'll get going.

13
A World of Zombies

プシーッ
PSSSHT

ザッ
ZHFF
ザッ
ZHFF

ヨリ
TEASE
ヨリ
TEASE

キュピーーン
SHEEEEEENG

Being a police officer means getting treated very poorly, right, Young Master?
I think my unit is special,
what with my boss being the way he is.

But it's your day off.

Though, in your case, Young Master,
it might be good since it'd let you take it easy in the mornings.
That'd be bad.

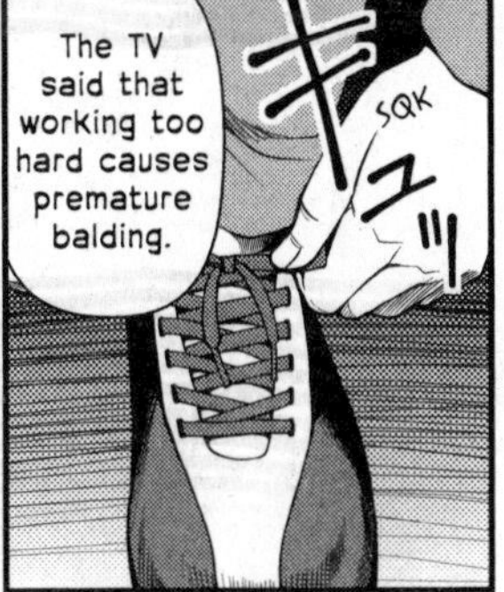
The TV said that working too hard causes premature balding.
キュッ
SQK

What is that supposed to mean, Mitsu?
HA HA HA HA HA HA HA
You spent an eternity gazing at the mirror
until your hair was perfect today!
Shut up!

What's the ruckus so early in the morning?
My apologies, Master Hiroki.

Morning, Hiroki.
Sorry to be so noisy.

There's no need to fuss over him, Mitsu.
He rejected the position that Father prepared for him and chose to become a cop instead.

It'd be one thing if he was career-track,
but he's just a lackey.

Thanks to that, every day is exciting.
That'd be impossible at Dad's company.

Now then, Mitsu,

I'm heading out.

There's no need to be,

she really is a beaut.

When I dropped by the love nest to say "Hi,"

she came scampering to the door going, "Bark, bark!"

BANG

That was my dog!

My wife was the one next to the animal, mature for her years, wearing ponytails.

WHUD

Ponytails!

But ya know, telling your wife to roll over in front of me was kinda—

BANG

Stop with the dog!

ははははははは
HA
HA
HA
HA
HA
HA

ははは
HA HA HA
HA HA HA
ははは
あはははは
HA-HA-HA HA-HA

Stand-up comedy
is better over here.

You're not very kind, Officer.
How many days has it been since I called you?
WHUMP

You might have been under surveillance.
Don't expect a date right away just 'cause you called.
Fair enough.

I had you shadowed for a while but there was no sign of a tail.
We should be fine.

Glad to hear it.
So,
will you believe me now?

About the world where you came from?
You said people don't revive, yet the population is 7 billion.
Who would believe such absurd non-sense?

How does the population grow to 7 billion without revival?
You're the one who said people die easily.
Ah, I see. So that's your reasoning.

There wouldn't be enough food or energy.
What sort of idiots would allow the population to grow so much without exercising control?
That is painfully correct, sir.

If you keep talking non-sense,
I can just hand you over to UNDO.
But from my perspec-tive, it's the reverse.
Anybody over here would think,
"This fatso is crazy."

You cure colds by shooting off your heads!
It goes so far beyond horror that it's hilarious!
ははは
HA HA HA
ははは
HA HA HA

It's as though all of mankind has been infected by zombies.
The crazy ones are this reality and you, its inhabitants.
ZWAKK

Hold on, Officer.
The humor doesn't end there.
SFF

For instance, that handgun that you carry...
Why does that sort of thing exist?

What are you getting at?

In our world, the gun is a tool for murder.
That's why our world is one where people ceaselessly kill each other with war and crime.

Guns are improved every year to become better tools for warfare,
but they aren't that different over here,
despite the fact that murder doesn't exist.

Y'know, Officer,
this world is strange in many ways besides "revival."

I have a few ques-tions.
Go ahead.

Do these "dentists" realy exist
in your world?

Oh, yeah... Of course.
There are plenty.
Too many, in fact. There are several in each town.

Are you familiar with the following acronym?
"JSDF."
It refers to the Japanese army.
There was no war here so they're still called the Japanese Army.

Huh? Hang on a minute...
Why do you know about the JSDF, Officer?

Your ears are quite sharp.
We caught him using the interrogation manual you sent us before.
Oh, was that helpful?

But I have a few questions about that manual...
I can't answer a single one.

There's a place filled with non-revivers like you.
The ones that cross over to here are called Vectors.
Good job, Officer! Glad you're quick on the uptake.

...
Anyways, is this an accurate explanation?

So how did you all get to Japan?
Hmm.
By ship? Plane?
I guess you could say I walked here...

Stop being so short-tempered.
"World" doesn't refer to a foreign country.
You're so thick-headed.

We'll work through that later.
Now it's your turn.
Tell me why you called me out here.

I want to sell you a Vector.

The organization has chosen my job.
I'm to be a realtor once again.

I'll hand that info over to you. In return, you let me walk.
Don't turn me over to UNDO even if I get arrested.

Yet another sleazy deal.
As expected of a man who killed 3 women so he could survive.
What are you talking about, Officer?
Didn't you send me back to the Escape Artists for just that purpose?

By the way, Kouda
If you hand us a load of crap, that's the end of it.

I'll answer
once I've seen your intel.

is now apprenticing with the Escape Artists.

Thanks for your continued support,
Officer.

Fine, you fat bastard.
The deal is on.

Aww. That was like...

I was listening in on my head-phones,
but the conversation was so erratic that I couldn't keep up.

人形町駅
A5
The Vectors came from another world?
What sci-fi novel is that from?

I don't think that he made it up.

Seven billion people sounds fake,
but it's likely that the Vector's society exists on that scale.
No way,
that is totally impossible!

If all we had was Takamiya's story, I wouldn't believe it, either.
But UNDO's manual
listed a key term, "JSDF,"
and he was able to define it as if it were common knowledge.

cialty Repair Shop
Maybe he knew what was in the manual...? No,
since he was caught because he knew what a "dentist" was.
If we assume that UNDO created that manual
based on knowledge of the Vectors' society,
then everything fits.

Whaat?! Chief, you believe Takamiya's story?
I'm not saying that.
But I can't eliminate the possibility.

SCHOO
CROSSIN
There's no point in thinking too deeply about it at this point.
But... really?
We still don't have all the puzzle pieces yet.

Scrape together even the most trivial information.
Do that, and the truth will reveal itself.

So cool!
BFFFT

...
You making fun of me?
Kids' Clothes
No, no, no!
I mean it!

Heh heh heh.
WHAP
ぱん
That's it!
A man's job has to be like this!

I'm glad
that I became a detective.
The hell's gotten into you...?
Ah, don't mind me.

Oh, yeah.
It's not 5 o'clock yet, but why don't we get a drink?
We're supposed to be off duty anyways.

I would be up for it,

but I have other plans.

You're 15 minutes late,

Lieutenant Kenzaki.

I told you I wasn't sure whether I'd make it.
I merely stated a fact. It wasn't criticism.
FaSo

This is why, Waka-bayashi.
Rain check.
Thanks for your hard work.

Ah ha ha ha! Roger!
Bye, Rin!
FaSoLaM
ALCOHOL

WHEW
ふうっ

First Takamiya, then Rin.
Chief sure is a workaholic.
くるっ
SPIN
OPEN

Don't let Kenzaki influence you.
Sorry, Shige,
but after seeing something like that ...
Oh ?

How now?

14
Cute Girl
ICER

TROMP
TROMP
SPLISH
Haa
Haa
Haa
Haa
Haa
ZWUP
ZPOP
ZWUP
We're at the stopover.
Repeat! We're at the stopover!
Good work. Can you see the clearing 200 yards to your northwest?
Yes, I can.
KLIK
VECTOR
VECT

ZSSH
SWOOP
That's the meet point. Head there immediately.
Roger! C'mon, let's go.
I don't think we're gonna make it.
VECTOR
OFFICER
RAT
TAT
TAT
TAT

BLAM
BLAM
BLAM
ZSSH
Eh hem!
Did you think that you could escape from the excellent Kiriko?
DAAZZLE

It's such a burden to be good at everything they make me do.
Damn it, Kiriko!
Are there any cops that can move with that much agility?!
Uh... So I can't do that?
Now we gotta start over, you dumbass!
Well of course she's pissed.
For real?!
RISE
KOFF
We all know that you're capable,
but this is training. We need you to act out your role.
KOFF
But there might be cops that can jump around and attack from above.
What, really?!
ZWUP
ZHAAAA
Of course there aren't!
Hurry up and start over!
GASHAK

An instructor and...

Who's that girl?

I hate remembering crap from my training days.
It's because I'm being forced to handle Kouda's training.

Looks like you're making progress with Kenzaki.
Sorry, Fuurin.
I've got orders to tail you.
Quietly spy on them!

We're talking about naïve Fuurin here,
so I doubt I'll spot them doing anything—
Huh?

WHISTLE
HOTEL

As I thought, we're being watched.

Yes. I felt someone respond to our kiss towards our six.
Might it be Sergeant Waka-bayashi?
Whoever it is, it doesn't bother me.

Well, I'm unhappy about it.
Why?

It says here that kissing while others look on can be stimulating,
but I didn't feel anything in particular.
Is that book really reliable?
All the Questions You Can't Ask, Answered!
Adult Dating

Plus, I really find the smell of cigarettes unpleasant.
That prevents me from proceeding to the next step.
What's next?

I will put my tongue in.
OK. Throw that book away.

WHAAMM

Fuurin kissed him?!
On this busy street?!
What the hell is going on?!

Where are they going, walking arm-in-arm?
Does that mean what I think it means? Does it?!

DIZZY
DIZZY
ぐるぐる
For real?! Wait a damn minute! Has she already seduced that greasy-haired dude?!
Is she as good in bed as she is with guns?!
Wow. They sure are showing off.

Makes me blush just watching them.
びくっ
JOLT

Oh, crap! I was too focused on Fuurin.
Y–You are...
どき どき
BADUM BADUM

Hey,
have we met somewhere ?
ばっ
WHAP

Well, not "met," but I've seen you before.
Where was it...?

That's right, at the college!
You're a student at Haruta College, right?
I remember thinking that you were a cute girl when I visited for work.
Oh... I see.
Crap crap crap crap crap crap crap.

Fancy meeting you here.
Are you shopping? With friends? Meeting someone?
Something like that. I'll be going now...
I gotta make my escape.

Oh, really! Let's chat until your friends get here.
The man who was kissing a girl over there is my boss.
O- Oh...?
Shut the hell up!

He's an old throwback with that greased-up hairdo, but he's like that now that he has a young girlfriend!
This guy is a cop with the Anti-Vector Unit.
Didn't he leave?!

She's just a plain, unsociable type who wears glasses,
so I never thought she'd be the type to kiss on a street in broad daylight.
I guess when you first start dating, it's hard not to get frisky.
If he just happened to spot me, that's one thing.
But if Fuurin is under suspicion and is being tailed, then that's a problem.
You look so cute wearing those glasses! So you like wearing your hair over your frames?
Which is it?

Which ...?
Let me get to the point.
I might not look it, but I'm a detective.

Here it comes!

Can I ask you something work-related?

Uhm, I have to go.

Huh? Just listen for a sec.

Is he buying time? If so, I should just...

Are you interested in a group date with some cops?

... What?

BLUSH
てれっ
I've always wanted to try a group date with college girls.
My workplace is nothing but guys.
Is he...
for real?!

I'm sure my coworkers would be thrilled.
Ah... Sorry, but...

Shit, I lost them.
I don't have the chance to meet anyone.
Please, help me out!

STAAARE

Uhm...
Did I make you mad?

My bad.
It's okay if you can't.
I mean, who'd wanna do a group date with cops?
SKRIT
SKRIT

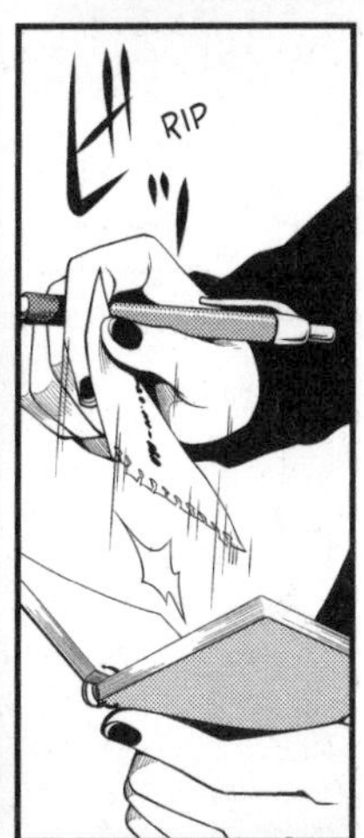
RIP

I don't think a group date is possible,
but here's my email.
What? Really?

Bye, Officer.
Might be able to get him to tell me about Kenzaki and Fuurin.
I'll keep him for now.

OK! I'll email you!
Once I'm done with him,

I can just kill him with RDS.

Phew.

Scrape together information,
and the truth will reveal itelf, right?

Oops.
VRRR
VRRR
Hello?
Hey, Waka-bayashi, where are you?

Ningyo-cho.
Huh? Are you with Kenzaki?
No, I'm working on my own.
Is there a new case?

Just got word of a man who was struck by a car and didn't revive.

A Vector ?!
No, it seems he had contracted RDS.

I'm currently checking his background and ID,
but everything seems to check out.

A witness said a woman was with him at the time of the accident,
but she vanished from the scene.

She may have been the Vector.
PLEASE CONSERVE PAPER
Shige, can the Anti-Vector Unit mobilize ?
Notice
I'm on it!

Kenzaki is on his way.
I'm going to question the victim's relations. Sorry, but could you—
Understood! I'll man the precinct!

I'm glad you're fired up, but your voice is too loud.
Sorry, Shige.

I'll leave it to you.

I wonder
why I've got a bad feeling about this.

Shige!
Ah, coming!

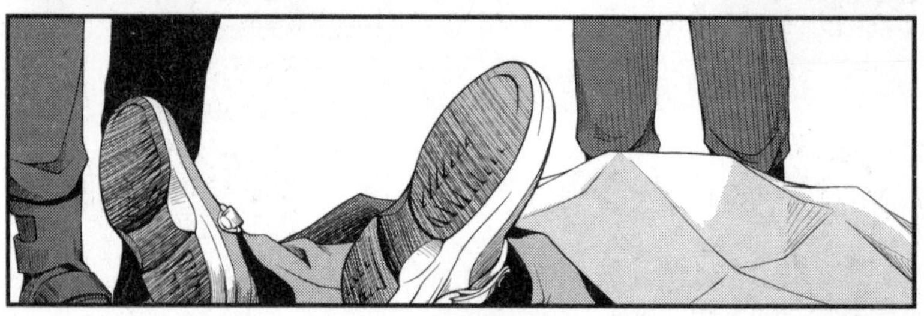

ピ ピ
PREET
PREET
ピー ッ
BIG SALE
FOOD
RICE
BIG
SALE
CIGARETTES
D V D

I got a text from my girl,
and was typing a response.
ポリ ポリ
SKRITCH
SKRITCH

I'm sorry.

I didn't realize someone was walking in front of me.
You can't use your phone while driving.

Ball Style HOTEL
FREE!!
Billiards/ Darts/ Sauna/ Food Service/ Internet And More!
HOTEL GAGA
HOTEL GAGA
The hotel district, huh.
MPD

Wonder if it was before or after he'd had his fun.
I feel sorry for him if it was before.
Uhm ...
the person that I hit was a Vector, right?

We're not sure yet.
Can you tell us about the girl he was with?
It happened so fast, I didn't really see her face.

From her outfit, I'd say she's a student.

キュッ
SQK
キュッ
SQK

So amazing.

He was quick to fall in love
and quick to die.

Guess this should do it.

And too quick to come.

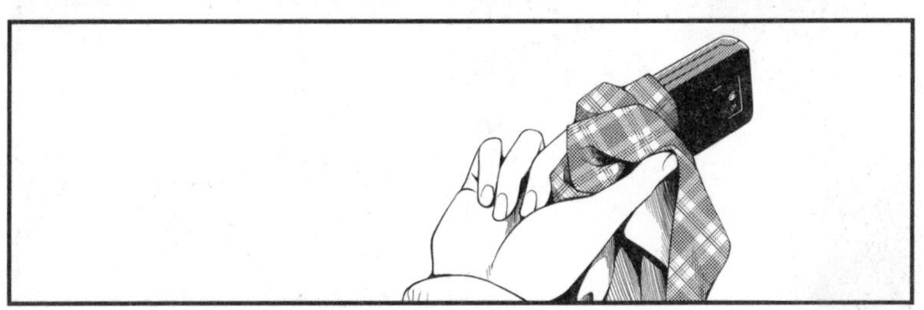

End of Chapter 14

15
The Vector Called Snow White

Tosshy is dead?

Your friend,

Toshimichi Oohashi, aka Tosshy,

We're in the process of investigating this as a Vector-related case.
This is the first time I've known someone with RDS.
Same here.
PREMIUM

Mr. Oohashi lived alone,
his cell phone has gone missing,
and he doesn't seem to have friends.

So we've decided to ask you, who were part of his clan* in an online game,
for any information, no matter how trivial, that you can supply us.
That's a tough one...

He was at a trade school, right?
But I don't think he went very often.
He would hole up in the arena starting at noon on weekdays.

Tosshy only talked about the game on Skype, too.
Never heard of any friends in his real life.
PREMIUM STEA
¥1800

* Clan: A group or team of online video game players, often used in fighting or first-person shooters. Similar to a "guild" in an MMORPG.

You did well to realize
that he had gaming friends, Shige.

The victim's computer was a gaming rig,
so when I signed into his account on an installed game,
I saw he was in a clan that I'd seen often in tournaments, so the rest was a snap.

I'm surprised
that you know so much about net games.
I don't compete anymore, but I still play co-op games.

And how did you figure out his password?
Oh, that? On his credit card statement was an order for pizza delivery, right—
Save it for later.

I don't care about the details.
The woman!
ふ
HOO
I want to know about the woman that Oohashi was with.

Are there any women who aren't here today that you all were close to?

List of Witnesses
CONFIDENTIAL
Handle name
Name, Address
Tosshy (@_@)
Bundori
Address: Unknown
Name: Unknown
What about this "Princess?" Isn't this a woman?

Pretty sure she's the sole woman in our clan.
She isn't here today because I couldn't get in touch with her.

Your name?
I'm Tobita.
I'm the captain of this clan.

What is she like?
Honestly she's not that good.
But she was really keen to learn, so I let her into the clan.

And now she's our clan's beloved idol—
I'm not talking about the game!

Her relation to Oohashi! Were they dating?
Ah, sorry about that.
But I really don't think they were a couple.

In fact, I once
asked the Princess out.

S-She turned me down, of course!
But the Princess told me then,

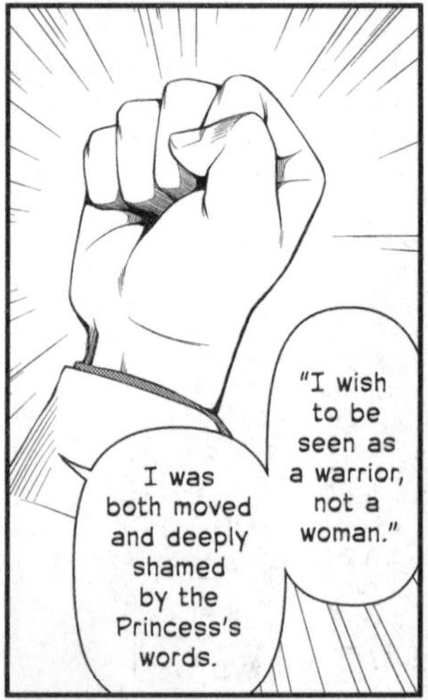
"I wish to be seen as a warrior, not a woman."
I was both moved and deeply shamed by the Princess's words.

"I hereby forbid romantic relations within this clan!"
By making the whole clan agree to this pact,
I answered the Princess's wish!

So Tosshy couldn't have been dating
the Princess, Officer.

Oh, so that's it? I was wondering why you suddenly banned
all romantic relation-ships.
aw shucks
Uhm...

テレッ
BLUSH
Sorry, Captain.
I'm dating the Princess.

SSK
スーッ

HOO
KLATTER
WHAAAAAT?!
We hit it off in a chat room.
It's been about two months.

That's how it is, Officer.
So Tosshy couldn't have been involved with the Princess.

That may be, but then...
Hold up.

What are you talking about?
I'm the Princess's boyfriend.

What?
What the hell are you talking about?
I'm not lying!
We just went on a date last week.

Uhm, well...
I'm dating the Princess, too.
ギョッ
SHOCK
What the heck is going on?

What... So, hang on, is she
three-timing?
Actually, I've been
dating her since last month...

For real? You shoulda told us!
But relationships were banned.
And she wanted to keep it a secret.

Waka-bayashi, contact UNDO.
Yes, sir.
Have all these guys tested for RDS.

Next question!

BIP ピッ

Who is the one who, in the middle of the night,

TWITCH ビクン
TWITCH ビクン
Ooh
Mmm... ...Ah

Heh heh.
HAA は一!
HAA は一っ
You did an expert job today.

Oh, I'm happy that you're finally satisfied.
SKFF
SKFF
What do you say we stop with the quizzes?

I don't really get them,
and the answer is always "me."

Let's take these off
and crank it up a notch already.

You told me not to be violent, and I wasn't.
C'mon, please?

Nope.

Ah!
SNATCH
ばっ
You have a wife and a child.

When did you...
Aww, I was tricked.

Well, I did think you were used to picking up women.
My mistake, my mistake.

Ah ha ha ha.
Let's just call this playtime
and have some fun.

What? No way.
I'll give you some cash.
Two... no, three hundred?

BANG
BANG
!!!
BANG

AAAAAAAAA
OOWWWWWWW

GRAAAAAAARGH

The fuck did you do, you little bitch?!
You fucking little bitch!!

I'm sorry
I didn't let you screw me.
God-damn bitch!
Hurry up and kill me already.
Listen,
I'm not the type to have sex without love.
Huh? What ...
See ya.
W-Wait, hey,
are you gonna just leave me here?
Wait.
I said wait...
Take care.

ぼ――…
DAAZE

I didn't think
that everyone but him caught RDS.

What happened to the infected?
They were all taken to UNDO's shelter.
It really is a shame.

Uhm...
JOLT
ビクッ
you were lucky not to have contracted it.

fngh...
カガっ
GRAB

Huh?
Uhh...
Uurrgh...
Bwuuhngnh...

Bwaaaaaaaaaaaaaagg
ちっ
TCH
Idiot.
Didn't need to say that.
Going by this situation, we can say with near certainty that the woman is the Vector.

Six points at once ...
If we include the first victim in the accident, that's seven.
We're dealing with a real monster.

You're granted revival at three points.
What do seven points get you?

Don't know.

Takamiya hadn't told me that much.

Seven points isn't the extent of that Vector's damage.

Hello, again.

Thank you for your hard work,

Tousai Precinct's Lieutenant Kenzaki.

There are 32 victims that we've confirmed.

She's a wicked Vector who's infected 39 people, including these new victims.

39...

She targets groups consisting exclusively of men.

She lets them dote on her, the lone woman of the group,
then when the time is ripe,
she gobbles up all of the fawning men.

As a man, I find her doubly hard to forgive.
May I ask a question?

Why are you sharing this information with us,
when you wouldn't tell us anything concerning Takamiya?

39 dwarves for one Snow White is too many, right?
It's time to put a stop to her havoc.
There's one more reason.

You outsmarted both UNDO and the Escape Artists
and shrewdly extracted info from Takamiya. We rate that highly.

I think the higher-ups will contact you soon.

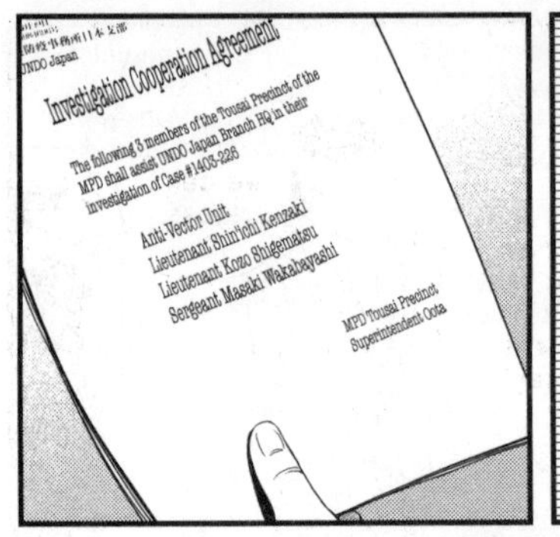
UNDO Japan
Investigation Cooperation Agreement
The following 3 members of the Tousai Precinct of the MPD shall assist UNDO Japan Branch HQ in their investigation of Case #1403-226
Anti-Vector Unit
Lieutenant Shin'ichi Kenzaki
Lieutenant Kozo Shigematsu
Sergeant Masaki Wakabayashi
MPD Tousai Precinct
Superintendent Oota

What does this mean?
Snow White's hunting grounds are online games and social media.
Arresting her will require swiftness and mobility.

But as you know,
as part of the UN, UNDO does not have the authority to investigate or make arrests.

Basically, we won't catch her if we have to get permission from the dimwitted police brass each time.
We need personnel that can respond right away.

If this is an order, then we can't refuse.
Come now, that isn't how this is, okay?
We need you to want to help us out.
If there are conditions for your cooperation, then tell me.

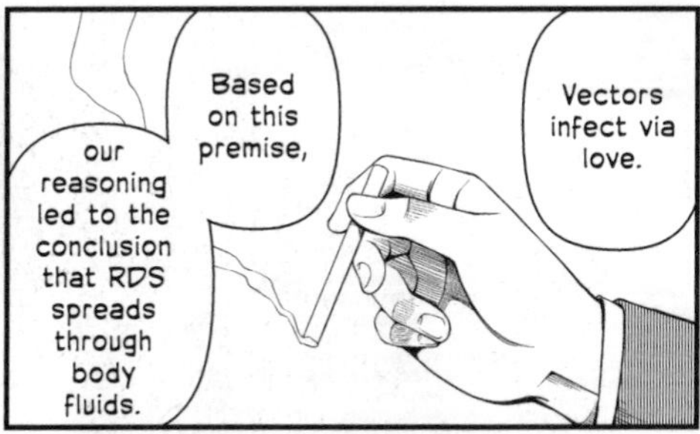
Vectors infect via love.
Based on this premise,
our reasoning led to the conclusion that RDS spreads through body fluids.

But then there was a case where a man contracted it without sexual contact.
I've been puzzling over it ever since.
Answer me this.

Is RDS
really an infectious disease?

End of Chapter 15